Writing Smarts

A Girl's Guide to Writing Great Poetry, Stories, School Reports, and More!

By Kerry Madden
Illustrated by Tracy McGuinness

★ American Girl™

Dedicated to . . .
Lucy, for her lovely imagination,
warm spirit, and laughing heart;
Flannery, for incisive comments, wit,
and honesty; Norah, for her light, joy,
and dancing fingers; and always . . .
for Kiffen

Published by Pleasant Company Publications

Copyright © 2002 by American Girl, LLC

Questions or comments? Call 1-800-845-0005,
visit our Web site at **americangirl.com**,
or write American Girl, P.O. Box 620497,
Middleton, WI 53562-0497

Printed in China.

06 07 08 09 10 C&C 15 14 13 12 11

American Girl™ and its associated logos are trademarks
of American Girl, LLC.

Editorial Development: Julie Williams, Michelle Watkins

Art Direction and Design: Camela Decaire

Production: Kendra Pulvermacher, Mindy Rappe

Illustrations: Tracy McGuinness

Photography: Jamie Young, Sandy May

**Magnetic Poetry is the property of Magnetic Poetry,
Inc. Used with permission.**

Library of Congress Cataloging-in-Publication Data
Madden, Kerry
Writing smarts : a girl's guide to writing great poetry,
stories, school reports, and more! / by Kerry Madden.
p. cm.
ISBN 1-58485-505-3
Creative writing (Elementary education)—Juvenile
literature. 2. English language—Composition and
exercises—Study and teaching (Elementary)—Juvenile
literature. 3. English language—Composition and
exercises—Juvenile literature. 4. Creative writing—
Juvenile literature. 5. Language arts (Elementary)—
Juvenile literature. I. Title.
LB1576 .M347 2002
372.62'3—dc21   2001058769

Dear Writer,

Maybe you've read something you've written and have thought, *"No way does that sound like me!"* Or you've stared at that big blank sheet of paper yawning on your desk and have asked, "What am I supposed to write?" Or you've written a story and have just wanted to make it better.

Here's a book to help you with all that. Discover how to be yourself when you write and how to keep the words flowing freely onto paper. Unlock the secrets to cooking up not just any story but *a good story.* Also, learn how to follow the paper trail to a great school report.

In this book you'll also get a handy guide to grammar, spelling, and punctuation, plus a pull-out deck of cards with creative sparks to beat writer's block. Now get ready to write smart!

Your friends at American Girl

Contents

LOVES

HATES

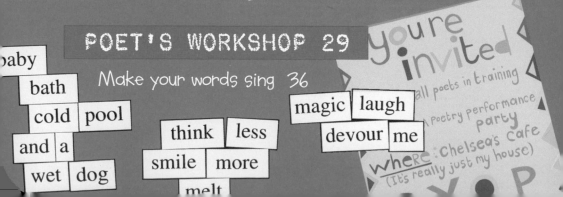

baby

bath

cold | pool

and | a

wet | dog

think | less

smile | more

melt

magic | laugh

devour | me

you're
invited

all poets in training

a poetry performance
party

where: Chelsea's cafe
(it's really just my house)

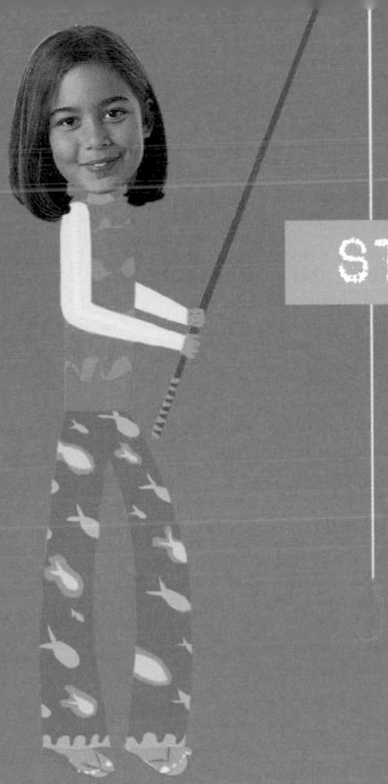

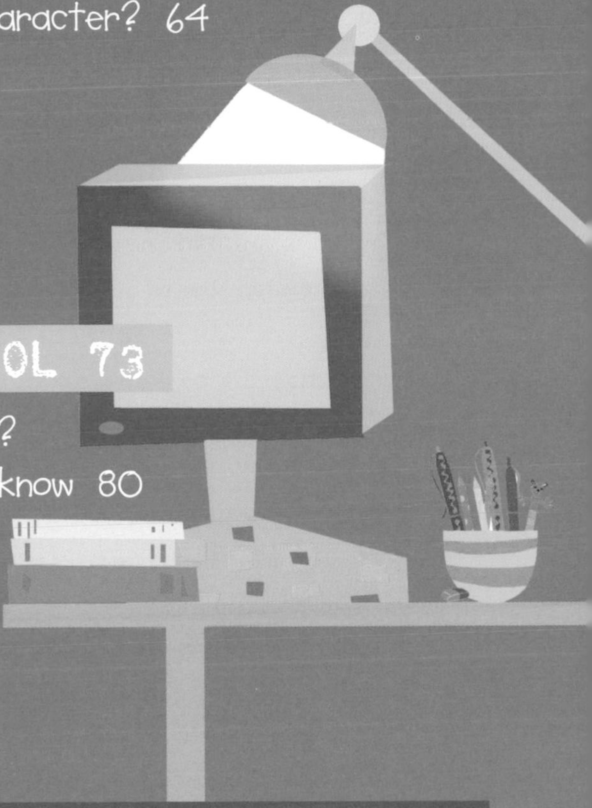

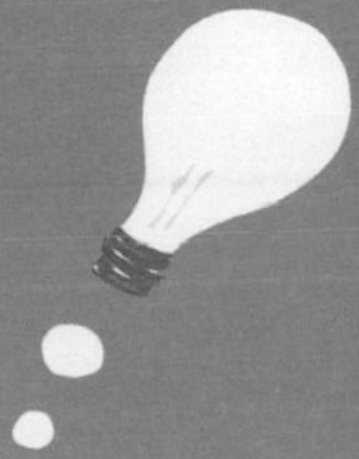

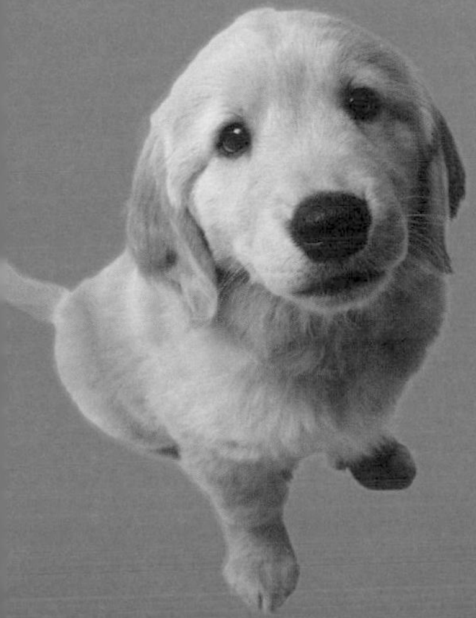

Ready to Write?

Circle the answer that describes what you'd do.

1. You want to write a story about a pioneer girl, but you're not sure where to start. You . . .

   a. Dig in the attic and find some old dress-up clothes. You put them on, walk around, and feel the scratchy fabric against your skin. Write it!
   b. Look up "pioneer girl" on the Internet and get side-tracked by clicking on all the links.
   c. Figure Laura Ingalls Wilder already wrote everything there is to know about pioneer girls, so you forget it.

2. You're supposed to write a poem for a contest. You . . .

   a. Go "people watching." You see a big man walking tiny dogs, a lady watering flowers in her bathrobe, and kids squealing on their bikes. Then you go home and write about what you saw.
   b. Make a list of words that rhyme, and get mad at yourself when you can't think of very many.
   c. Tell yourself you'll never win and blow it off.

3. Your teacher asks you to write a story from the point of view of your dog or your cat or your pet iguana. You . . .

    a. Write: "Look at those greedy humans, stuffing their faces while I eat canned mush ON THE FLOOR!"

    b. Begin your story: "I'm really not a dog, but if I were a dog, I would be a Lab because they like to swim."

    c. Bite your pencil and say, "How am I supposed to know what a dog thinks?" You watch TV for inspiration.

4. Your mom is making you keep a journal of your summer vacation. You . . .

    a. Begin: "All I see from the backseat of this van are signs to buy fireworks. Dad won't stop the car. Mom keeps singing to oldies on the radio. . ."

    b. Scribble: "What a waste of time. This summer is going to be so boring. It's a million degrees outside and she wants me to write about it? I want to forget it!"

    c. Announce: "No way! I don't lead an interesting life! But I wouldn't mind a Game Boy for the road."

5. You have to write a report on the Pony Express, so you . . .

    a. Visit the stables to find out what it would have been like to ride a horse for 70 miles straight.

    b. Look up the topic in the encyclopedia and reword what is written there.

    c. Check out books with pretty pictures of horses but then realize that none of them say anything about the Pony Express. You turn the paper in late and get points taken off.

PONY EXPRESS

Writer's Workshop

Count how many of each letter you circled to find out whether or not you're a ready writer!

Mostly a's
Sharp and Ready!

Your willingness to try new adventures will feed your stories. You're a good listener and observer of life, and you're not likely to quit before you have the words down on paper.

Mostly b's
Scratchy

You're on the right track, but sometimes you don't trust yourself. Don't worry too much about what other people might think. Follow your heart and write what's in your head.

Mostly c's
Dull

O.K., it's high time to put a STOP to the little voice inside your head that says, "Who do you think you are? You can't do it!" Ignore that voice and let your pen fly with the words, "YES, I CAN!"

Now let's get writing . . .

A Tree of One's Own

Scope out a quiet place to write—a place where you can stop and listen to your voice.

on the back steps

under the covers

in a cozy attic

in the backseat of the car on a roadtrip

up in a tree

sprawled out in the grass

perched on the front porch

swinging in a breezy hammock

at the top of the slide

next to the clothes dryer

in the bubble bath

Tune Out & Tune In

Even if you can't find a quiet place to write, you can still train your brain to shut out the noises around you— the TV blaring, a dog barking, the baby crying. Just close your eyes and try to focus. The words will come to you.

Get Equipped!

Whether you write on paper or on a computer, keep these writer's tools by your side.

pencil sharpener

Post-its

dictionary

synonym finder
or thesaurus

erasers

library
card

Thinker Toys

Keep your hands busy the next time you stop to think about what to write. Slide a slinky around or scrunch a stress ball.

lucky pencil

... scissors for cutting

tape for pasting

Idea Catcher

You never know when a good idea will strike you. And when one does, you may think you'll remember it because it's *so good!* But in reality you probably won't. What's the solution? Keep an idea notebook with you at all times to capture those great ideas that inspire you.

A-muse Yourself

Find a muse—something that or someone who inspires you to write.

Your muse might be your imaginary friend from childhood, a picture of a cute puppy, or your favorite stuffed animal. Think of it as a friend, coach, and cheerleader who says, "Write, girl, write!"

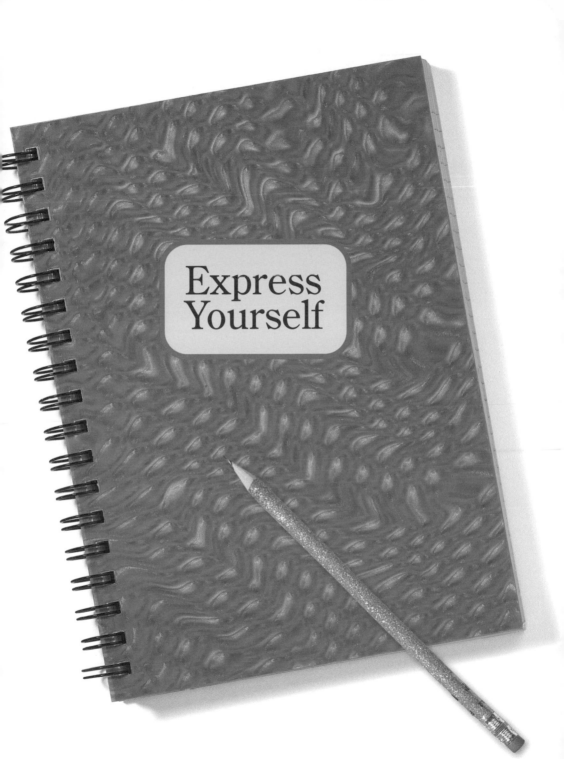

Express
Yourself

Find Your Voice

Every writer has her own voice—her own way of expressing her thoughts, ideas, and feelings.

YOU have a unique voice. In fact, nobody else in the world has **your** voice. Nobody can tell a story or write a report quite the way **You** can.

So, how do you find your voice? Where is it hiding?

Look in your heart and in your head.

L♥VES

What gets you giddy with delight?

What expands your heart with love?

What fires up your pulse?

Write from

Make a list of your loves and hates, fancies

HATES

What whips you into a white hot rage?

What sends bone-chilling goose bumps down your spine?

What makes you cry bitter tears?

Your Heart

and fears, right inside this big beating heart.

Big Dragon

Look back at your loves and hates heart, and read all your words of joy, fear, sorrow, and rage. Is there a story behind each love and hate?

I am mad, roaring-dragon mad, when my brother pitches me balls too fast for batting practice the driveway, and I tell him over and over to stop, and he doesn't listen, and then he throws the ball hard, and it hits me in the elbow, and I wish I co sprout humongous wings and fly at him and pic him up by the scruff of his unwashed neck and ZOOOOOOOOOM over the sky with his skinn not-listening body and drop him into a volca full of spewing purple and red bubbling lava . .

You probably wouldn't really want to drop that annoying brother into a volcano, but when you write about it, you can channel your anger by letting it all out. Even better, you have the beginning of a story with conflict, passion, and flying dragons.

Emotions!

Write about one of your big dragon emotions.

_____

_____

_____

_____

_____

_____

_____

_____

_____

_____

_____

_____

_____

_____

_____

Dear Diary

A diary is the perfect place to write what's in your heart. In your diary, you should feel comfortable writing about any subject *under the sun*, from what you had for breakfast to your first crush.

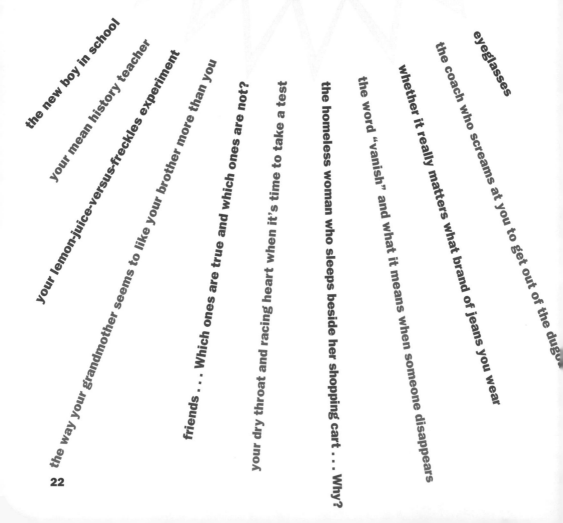

the new boy in school

your mean history teacher

your lemon-juice-versus-freckles experiment

the way your grandmother seems to like your brother more than you

friends . . . Which ones are true and which ones are not?

your dry throat and racing heart when it's time to take a test

the homeless woman who sleeps beside her shopping cart . . . Why?

the word "vanish" and what it means when someone disappears

whether it really matters what brand of jeans you wear

the coach who screams at you to get out of the dugout

eyeglasses

You Name It

Some girls like to name their diaries. Anne Frank called her diary "Kitty." She began each entry, "Dear Kitty..." Other kids have used "Dear Grasshopper" or "Dear Cherry Blossom in Spring." Others don't use any name at all. There is no right or wrong way. Do what feels right to you.

Secret Starters

I've been **meaning** to tell you this . . .

You'll never **guess** what happened today . . .

Here's what's **bugging** me . . .

Last night I **dreamed** . . .

Dear Diary

I've been meaning to tell you this for a long time. I Like somebody, and his name is PHIL. He has blond hair and hazel green eyes. He is very generous and nice, because yesterday he gave me his lunch money because I forgot mine at home. He plays basketball, and I try to play, too, but it doesn't really work, because I'm horrible. But sometimes I get lucky and make a shot. Sometimes I just like to play. I think about him

Write What You Think

What are you thinking about right now—this very moment? Does one thought lead to another and then to another? That is how "stream of consciousness" works in writing. Imagine an icy stream of water flowing over mountain rocks. As the water travels downstream, the water gushes forth in some places, and in other places it s-l-o-w-s to a ripple. The stream of water is like the stream of thoughts in your head—sometimes they come fast and sometimes they trickle.

Just write with the flow.

If you fight it, you're likely to get frustrated.

Pick Your Brain

Choose a subject to contemplate.* Then put your pencil to the paper, and keep up with your thoughts, ideas, observations, and reflections.

Try it!

BIG Truth

You have something to say.

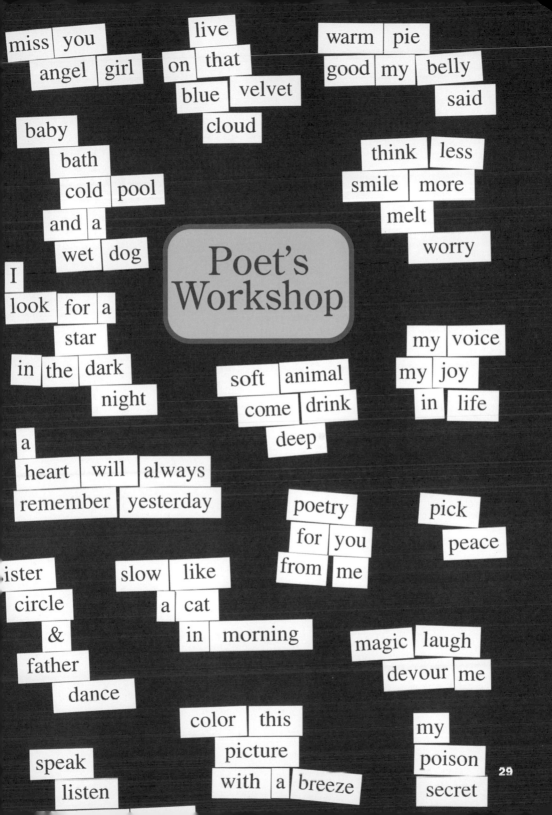

miss you
angel girl

live
on that
blue velvet
cloud

warm pie
good my belly
said

baby
bath
cold pool
and a
wet dog

think less
smile more
melt
worry

I
look for a
star
in the dark
night

Poet's
Workshop

my voice
my joy
in life

soft animal
come drink
deep

a
heart will always
remember yesterday

poetry
for you
from me

pick
peace

ister
circle
&
father
dance

slow like
a cat
in morning

magic laugh
devour me

color this
picture
with a breeze

speak
listen

my
poison
secret

29

A Poet's Path

Start
with a thought, an idea, or a feeling that you want to capture.

Pick
a format.

acrostic
limerick
ballad
couplet
haiku
lyric

To rhyme . . .

You can catch a fish
Or polish a dish
But never, ever
Squish a wish!

To rhyme, pick words with similar sounds. You can place rhymes at the end of every line, at the end of every other line, or even within a line.

. . . or . . .

Not to rhyme . . .

She climbs staring
Over branches and apples
Grabbing fruit
Then leaps down.

Free verse is written without rhyme or a repeating rhythm, which means that words don't have to sound alike and lines don't have to have the same number of beats.

Choose the right words

to capture your thoughts, feelings, or vision. Play with familiar words or search for new ones. Mix and match them to see how they work together.

Make line breaks.

Decide where each line of your poem should end. It can be at a natural pause, to emphasize a certain thought or word, or to create a specific rhythm. Do whatever works for you!

Read it aloud!

The sounds of the words and their rhythm should be music to your ears.

A Note on Rhythm

The sounds that words make create a rhythm, called *meter*. Each syllable—stressed or unstressed—is a beat.

Three brothers are fine,
And that's what I've got
But having a sister
Would sure hit the spot!

Come to Your Senses

Great poetry captures feelings, thoughts, or scenes with words.

I see . . .

A pile of dirty clothes on the floor . . .
The sun spilling across my bedspread . . .
Freckles on my arms . . .

_____

_____

I hear . . .

Mom singing . . . My brother yelling, "Where are my stupid socks?" . . .

_____

_____

What do you . . .

see,

hear,

smell,

taste,

and feel

at this very moment?

Write it down.

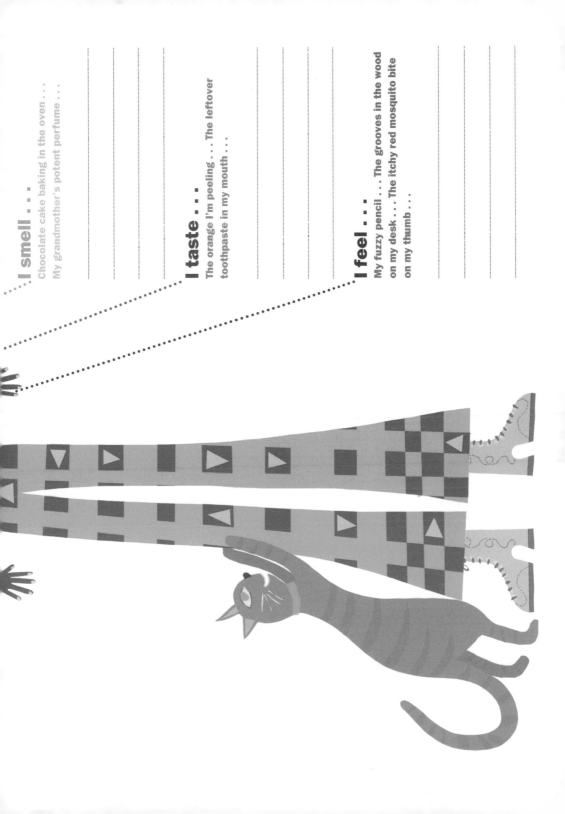

I smell . . .

Chocolate cake baking in the oven . . .
My grandmother's potent perfume . . .

I taste . . .

The orange I'm peeling . . . The leftover
toothpaste in my mouth . . .

I feel . . .

My fuzzy pencil . . . The grooves in the wood
on my desk . . . The itchy red mosquito bite
on my thumb . . .

Capture It

Parachute Girls Say

Parachute girls warn
The jump steals your stomach
The swirling sky eats your breath
Ice cold air awakens you
Plummeting tears your nerves
You freeze in midair
When your parachute opens

The floating gives you back your stomach
The blue sky returns your breath
Warm fresh air relaxes you
Slow descent pastes your nerves back on
When you land on the fresh sweet ground

You listen in the empty fields
Where you have come from
You realize that no matter where you land
You have touched the sky
—Flannery, California

Now try to capture your own senses in a poem.

Make Your Word

Choosing the right words can make your writing sing. It's all in the way you play with them!

New & Improved!

**Tired of using the same old words?
Add some zing!**

argue	quibble
cheat	swindle
circle around	orbit
copy	mimic
cry	wail
eat	gobble
grab	snatch
fly	soar
lean over	slump
lose	squander
make fun of	lampoon
mix	jumble
move fast	zip
pick on	pester
ring	chime
ruin	spoil
satisfy	quench
shake	tremble
shine	dazzle
smash	pulverize
sleep	snooze
talk too much	yammer
trick	bamboozle
won't sit still	squirm

**Pluck your dictionary or
thesaurus for more zing!**

Sing

Alliteration Generation

Alliteration happens when you repeat the beginning consonant sounds of words. If you've ever rattled off a tongue twister, you know that alliteration makes it just plain fun to say the words!

Gabby grabbed her great guitar.

Fill in the blanks with L and S words.

Lovely L_____ lies

On the l_____ lake

L_____ to l_____ l_____.

Sweet S_____ strives

To s_____ and s_____

On Saturdays and S_____.

Assonance Dance

Assonance happens when vowel sounds— long E, short U, etc.—repeat.

Gabby had a nap after that.

The lucky duck mucked about in the mud.

Kim hid her tin of pickles.

Sam sat in the sand and snacked on apples.

More Ways to

Simile Show

A simile is a comparison of two things using "like" or "as."

Your turn:

Screech like a _____ .

As happy as a _____ .

Fly like a _____ .

As silly as a _____ .

Float like a _____ .

Sting like a _____ .

Howl like a _____ .

As soft as a _____ .

Annie is like a daisy
Cheerful and bright
With arms open wide
She drinks in the light.

Rock Your Words

Metaphor Jam

A metaphor compares two subjects or ideas without using "like" or "as." Metaphors are a little harder to write than similes, but usually pack more punch.

My mom is my guardian angel always standing behind me in whatever I do.

Metaphor Maker

Answer each question with a special someone in mind. Then expand each answer into a poem.

1. If she were a color, which one would she be?

2. What kind of gem would she be: A red-hot ruby or a glowing pearl?

3. What kind of food: Warm, soft mashed potatoes? A bubbly soda?

4. What article of clothing: Easy-going sneakers? A sparkly shirt?

Sound Check

Punch up your poetry with noisy words like these examples of onomatopoeia.*

* buzzword **Onomatopoeia** (ah-na-mah-ta-PEE-a): words that sound just like what they describe

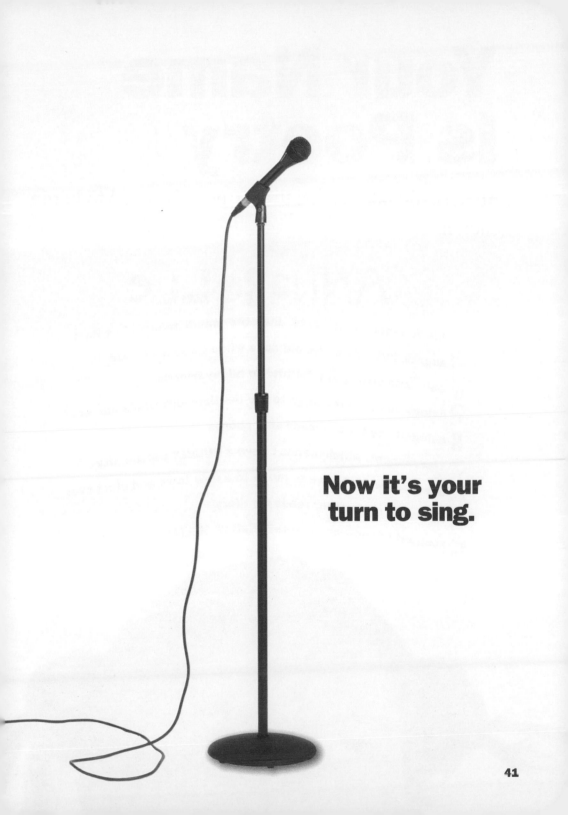

Now it's your turn to sing.

Your Name Is Poetry

An acrostic poem uses the letters of a word to begin each line.

ANNaBeLLe

A ble to rescue dogs, cats, and other small animals in a flash

N aughty, but only in the old days when I was a wee kid

N oble *and strong and faithful to all my friends

a nxious when I have to go to the dentist—but who's perfect?

B esieged *by far too many silly chores

e ffervescent, which means I have a BUBBLY personality

L onesome when I have to move to a new town and start over

L ivid when my brother reads my diary

e xcellent friend—any takers? Hello? HELLO?

Use the letters in your name to write an acrostic poem about yourself. Spell your first name down the first column, then start each line with a word that begins with the letter on that line.

buzzword **Besieged:** pressured, nagged, hounded, bothered

buzzword **Noble:** kingly, queenly, famous, honored

Make a Wish

Write a poem to describe your biggest wish.

I wish I could ride a unicorn
I'd fly up to the clouds
At night I'd catch
One billion stars
And hum a tune out loud.
I'd fly across the rainbow,
I'd fly above the sea.
I'd make friends with bees and butterflies
And ask them out to tea.
—Brittany, **Michigan**

hey, nice metaphor!

Awesome assonance!

I wish I had
A crown of butterflies
An ocean of smiles
A ribbon of fire
A meadow of quiet
A tree of hearts
A sun of dandelions
A window of wind
A bouquet of clouds
And a world of peace.
—Katie, **New York**

Haiku Heaven

A haiku (HIGH-koo) is a Japanese form of poetry. Each haiku has three lines and a total of seventeen syllables—five syllables on the first line, seven on the second, and five on the third.

Say this poem out loud while counting the syllables. Hear the rhythm?

```
An-gel in blue skies
 1   2   3    4     5
Float-ing on a fluf-fy cloud
  1     2   3 4  5   6    7
Whis-per in my ear
  1    2   3   4   5
```

Write your own haiku on the clouds below.

Take a Number

Create a poem based on your best friend's birth date, your phone number—even Mom's license plate!

Birthday Poem

Don't know what to get your best friend for her birthday? Write a poem using her birth date to determine how many syllables will go on each line.

December 17, 1991 = 12/17/91

Month (12)

1   You

2   Are great

Day (17)

1   You

7   Make me want to laugh out loud

Year (91)

9   I'll never have a better friend than

1   You

License to Rhyme

Write a rhyming poem based on the letters and numbers of a
license plate. Great for road trips!

S ....
(start the line with an "s")

W ....
(start the line with a "w")

W ....
(start the line with a "w")

3 ....
(use 3 syllables)

1 ....
(use 1 syllable)

3 ....
(use 3 syllables)

Phone Poem

Write your telephone number in the blue circles below. Then write a
poem using the same number of syllables as the number on each line.

For example, if your telephone number is 555-3432, put 5 syllables in the first line, 5 in the

second, 5 in the third, 3 in the fourth, and so on.

Sing Along . . .

Combine poetry with music and you've got a song!

See for yourself . . .

Sing this poem to the tune of "Twinkle, Twinkle, Little Star":

```
Freeze pops, ice cream, lemonade
Pools and hammocks in the shade,
No more book reports or tests,
Science, history, or recess.
This is my idea of cool—
It's what we call the end of school!
—Kassie, Texas
```

Rap to Remember

Rap songs are rhyming poems spoken to a beat. Write your own rap about things that you've seen and done—or to memorize important facts for school.

```
Who's That Girl?
She was a scientist
Don't you know?
She studied radium
And watched it glow
She won the Nobel Prize
But not only that
She won it TWO times
And that's a fact!
```

Answer: Marie Curie

50

Listen to a favorite song and write down the lyrics—
or make up your own to go along with the beat!

Poetry Slam!

you're
invited

who: all poets in training

what: A poetry performance party

where: chelsea's cafe
(It's really just my house)

B. Y. O. P.
(Bring your own poem)

Before the party, record your poems in a poetry notebook. Practice reading them aloud—syllable by syllable, line by line—emphasizing special words and keeping the rhythm as you go. Then get together with friends who have done the same and read your poems aloud. Vote on most awesome alliteration, rhyme queen, best beat, and more!

Story
Catcher

Go Fish!

You are a story catcher, and the creatures gliding beneath the ripples are the hundreds of stories swimming around in your head. Throw out your line to see what you can catch!

the stupidest thing you ever did

a really great photograph

a lesson well learned

Today's Catch Which type of tale will you hook?

Fiction a made-up story

Nonfiction a story about something that really happened

Historical Fiction a story that takes place during a specific time in history

Science Fiction a story about science's effect on society, often in the future

Fantasy a story about magical characters and imaginary worlds

Biography a true story of a person's life written by someone else

Autobiography a true story of a person's life written by the person

Memoir a true story by a person writing about a period of time in her life

Fairy Tale a make-believe story, often with dragons, fairies, dwarfs, and princesses

Myth a historical tale or fantasy that is used to explain the nature of things

Fable a story with a moral or lesson to be learned

Play a story written for the stage, with live actors performing the story

Screenplay a story written for the movies or television

that silly thing your pet does

a "pinch me, I'm dreaming" day

a scary animal

a beautiful dream

the best present you ever got

the strangest day ever

Cook Up a Story

SOUP STORY

Ingredients

2 cups characters 1 cup setting
1 cup conflict 1 teaspoon juicy details

Plot

1. Combine characters and setting over low heat.
2. Stir in conflict and let simmer.
3. Add more conflict and juicy details, turn up the heat,
   and bring to a boil.
4. Do a taste test. You'll know it's done
   when the conflict is dissolved.

BASIC RECIPE

The three little pigs

Ingredients

1 straw house 3 little pigs who can't agree
1 stick house 1 huffy, puffy, hungry wolf
1 brick house

Plot

1. Once upon a time, there were three pigs who couldn't agree on what
   material to build their house with, so they decided to each build their own
   kind of house.
2. Along came a big bad wolf who was hungry for some chubby pigs.
3. The wolf blew down the first little pig's straw house. The first pig ran to the
   second pig's stick house. The wolf followed and blew down the second pig's
   house. The two pigs ran to the third pig's brick house. The wolf followed.
4. The wolf huffed and puffed but couldn't blow down the brick house.
5. The three little pigs won!

BONUS RECIPE

Now follow the basic recipe to create your own story.

YOUR RECIPE

(Title)

Ingredients

(Title)

Plot

(Title)

What's Your Problem?

Create a big problem, or conflict, for your character to struggle with throughout your story, and you'll have your readers hooked till the end.

The Story Arc

Plan when to throw bumps and hurdles in your character's path.

Beginning

Introduce the problem. What does your character want . . . or not want? What is in her way? What troubles her?

Problem—the big "thing" that your character has to deal with or overcome
- Divorce
- Being the new kid and fitting in
- Finding something she's good at
- Making the grade

Middle

Add bumps along the way that make the character rise to the challenge of . . .

Bumps—those little "things" that get in your character's way
- House for sale
- Finding a place to sit at lunch
- Superstar sister wins yet another trophy
- Pop quiz

. . . The biggest hurdle of all!

This is the moment of greatest conflict. It is the point in the story when your character has to deal with or overcome the big problem that you set up at the beginning of the story.

Hurdles—the trouble has reached its highest point
- Dad gets remarried
- New "friends" dump you
- Basketball tryouts
- Big "make-or-break" test

End

The conflict is solved. Your character either gets what she wants or she doesn't. Or she could get what she wants only to discover she doesn't want it after all. Whatever the case, your character has changed or learned something.

Eyes on the Prize—what your character earns or learns
- Two families are better than none
- A true friend forever
- Pride in herself
- Honor roll

BIG Truth

It pays to be original.

Stay away from characters, plots, or phrases that are overused or are not your own. The prince rescuing the sleeping princess is old news to your readers. Give them something new!

Nothing biting?

Live Bait

Nibble on one of these story starters.

What if your best friend's mom caught you snooping in her attic?

What if your two best friends suddenly decided they hated each other?

What if you found a mysterious key?

What if your cat could talk—but only you could hear her?

What if you were invited to a slumber party—at the haunted house down the street?

What if your braces picked up secret radio transmissions from outer space?

What if you rescued an injured dolphin?

What if your baby sister had super powers?

What if your mom and dad were Santa's elves?

What if you found the cure for freckles?

What if you had a magic ring that made you invisible?

What if a UFO landed in the school parking lot?

What if your brother started being nice to you all of a sudden?

What if your favorite star knocked on your door one day?

What if a family of monsters moved in next door?

What if your life were filmed 24 hours a day, 7 days a week?

What if you found a secret passageway behind your bookcase?

What if you ran for president—and won!?

What if you found a four-leaf clover?

What if a genie popped out of your soda can and granted you three wishes?

What if you found a baby dinosaur egg in your mom's new exotic plant?

What if a friend told the whole school who you have a crush on?

What if you found a map to buried treasure?

What a Character!

How to Create a Great Character

1. **Paint a picture** of her and her world. Put believable words in her mouth. This will help the reader get an idea of what the character looks like, what she sounds like, and where she lives.

2. **Give her some personality!** Reveal what she loves and hates so that the reader can understand how she sees the world.

3. **Make her unique!** Avoid stereotypes ✳ like "cute little girl," "old man," or "pretty woman." Instead, make up original descriptions like "the kid with the skinned knees who sucked spaghetti through her straw and popped her bony knuckles every hour."

4. **Motivation** is what makes a character behave in a certain way. Make it clear to readers why your character does the things she does. For example, if she's an only child, she could yearn for a sister.

✳ **buzzword Stereotype: routine, cliché, overused phrase or idea, unoriginal**

with *Your* Character!

Take your character out to lunch and ask her a few questions.

1. What is her favorite color?
   a. Black   b. Pink   c. CRIMSON
   d. other _____

2. What is her favorite food?
   a. fruit pizza   b. tofu meatloaf   c. egg quesadillas
   d. other _____

3. How does she eat an Oreo cookie?
   a. dunks it in milk until it's soggy
   b. pulls it apart and scrapes the white stuff off
      with her teeth
   c. crushes it up and puts it on top of ice cream
   d. other _____

4. What does she *hate-hate-hate* to do?
   a. dishes   b. take out trash   c. get called on in class
   d. other _____

5. Where does she live?
   a. in an Airstream trailer on the lot of a movie set
   b. in a high-rise apartment with a great view
   c. under a mushroom in the forest
   d. other _____

6. What kind of weather does she like best?

    a. thunderstorms in the middle of the night

    b. snowflakes as big as her fist

    c. when it's rainy and sunny at the same time—a rainbow day

    d. other _____

7. What secret place does she go to when she is angry?

    a. attic   b. basement   c. tree

    d. other _____

8. How would she describe herself?

    a. **BRAVE**   b. Kooky   c. hot-Tempered

    d. other _____

9. Where would she like to travel?

    a. China   b. Nashville   c. North Pole

    d. other _____

10. What does she do when she gets nervous?

    a. twirls her hair   b. talks fast   c. stutters

    d. other _____

11. What can't she resist?

    a. a good joke   b. kittens   c. marshmallow fluff

    d. other _____

12. Special powers?

    a. math whiz

    b. answers the phone even before it rings

    c. contagious smile

    d. other _____

Feel like you know her better?

Good! Now write about her.

1. Describe her world. Don't forget the details!

_____

_____

_____

2. What does she love? Hate?

_____

_____

_____

3. Why does she do the things she does? What does she want?

_____

_____

_____

4. What makes her different from anyone else?

_____

_____

_____

Chitchat

The Do's and Don'ts of Dialogue

Do use dialogue to move the story along, give clues about characters, and set the mood. Cut any useless chatter.

Don't forget how your character feels at a certain point in the story. If she's excited, she might squeal, "Way to go!" If she's mad, she might snap, "No!"

Do place punctuation marks inside quotation marks. "Hey!" she cried. NOT "Hey"! she cried.

Don't lose track of who says what. Make sure it's clear to the reader who is speaking.

Do read dialogue aloud to make sure it sounds natural.

Don't make all your characters talk the same way. Give each a favorite expression, like "cute!" or "hon," and speech patterns, like "like" or "um."

Do be true to what your character would really say. A ten-year-old girl would say, "That's cool." But her grandmother would say, "That's nice."

Try It!

Fill in the speech bubbles with your own dialogue.

Psst!

Secret Story Ingredient: Details

The sights, sounds, smells, tastes, and textures of a story's make a good story great.

Details make your story stick.

When you finish a draft of your story, put it away and then come back to it a day or two later with fresh eyes. Read the story aloud to yourself and look for spots where you can add details. Maybe the ice cream in your first draft didn't have a flavor. Give it one. Maybe the soccer field you wrote about didn't have a smell. Add it.

Bubble gum   always
∧ice cream∧makes her smile.

        gobbled   cold, greasy
She∧ate∧the∧french fries.
                       ∧
                    that had fallen to the
                    bottom of the McDonald's bag

Done?

Not until you've answered these questions.

1. Do I give readers a clear picture of my characters?

   YES   NO

2. Do I describe the setting clearly?

   CRYSTAL CLEAR   A BIT MURKY

3. Does the story get boring or slow down in some places?

   NEVER!   Kind of

4. Do I repeat the same word or ideas too often?

   NOPE   Ummm...

5. Is anything confusing or unclear?

   no   don't think so

6. Do I leave out important parts?

   NOPE   OOOPS!

7. Is the conflict or problem in the story solved?

   YES   not really

8. Do I show how the main character changes or what she learns?

   YES   un-uh

9. Are all the loose ends tied up by the end of the story?

   OF COURSE   I forgot!

Write for School

The 19th Amendment

Lucy Madden-Lunsford
November 13, 2001
Social Studies

BIG
Truth

Reports are just good stories.

Find something interesting that you want to
say by looking in your heart or your head.
Do you think marigolds are the coolest
flowers ever? Or is it hard to believe that
women weren't allowed to vote until 1919?
Write about it!

Like a good story, A gREAt rEpOrt has a . . .

Beginning

Tell us what you're going to talk about.

Hook your reader with a strong opening statement. Remember what first captured your attention about the subject. Make that the big idea—or premise—of your report.

middle

Tell it.

In the middle of your paper, write what you know about the subject. Each paragraph should back up the big idea you presented in the beginning. Don't forget to add details that stick!

End

Tell us what you told us.

Make a final point. Mention your big idea again and summarize what you said in the middle.

The 19th Amendment

The 19th Amendment allowed women to vot first time. Before 1919, women belonged to m property like chickens or a house. They didn same rights as men. Two best friends, Elizabe Stanton and Susan B. Anthony, decided to work voting rights.

Stanton and Anthony worked for fifty y to give women the vote. They had a big fight them. Since men were the head of the family, thought their vote should count as their wiv Men didn't want their wives to vote. Even c thought women should not vote, but Stanton a knew women should have their own voices in a booth. They formed the NWSA – the National Suffrage Association. Many other women join still couldn't vote. They had to get the wo women gave speeches at noisy movies during They also protested in the crowded streets. ple began to understand why women should vc

Stanton and Anthony got old, so new take over the fight for women to vote. Fi Congress passed the 19th Amendment and wom were able to vote. Women learned they were property of their husbands. They could vot anybody else.

NWSA   VOTE

Loved It!

Hated It!

Book Reports Made Easy!

Have a book report due? Think like a critic.

You'll love some books while others may send you howling, "Never again!" Whether it's two thumbs down or a four-star rating, think about why you feel the way you do. Be ready to back up your statements with examples from the book.

The 5 Ws

A great book report will answer questions like the ones below:

Character
Who are the people (animals, talking mailboxes) in the story? Which character in the book interested you the most? Why?

Plot
What is the action of the story? What part of the story made you gasp with disbelief or fear or delight? What was the main problem or challenge?

Setting
Where and When does the story take place? At any point while reading, did you wish you could jump into the book and taste the dinner cooking on the stove? What details do you remember the most?

Theme
Why did the author tell this story? What main idea or message comes across at the end of the story? Did a certain part make you think about or reflect on your own life?

Keep a list of favorite and not-so-favorite books here.

Prove It!

Want your writing to persuade others to agree with you? Give them facts to support your opinions.

Here's what I think!

Hannah F
Englis
December 3, 200

Girl on the Throne

In December 2001, Japan ecstatically greeted the birth of a long-awaited child, Aiko, born to th Crown Prince and Princess. This baby is next in an unbroken Imperial family line that began in 660 B.C This only child of the Emperor's eldest son should inherit what is called the Chrysanthemum Throne. T only problem is, the baby is a girl!

The 1889 Japanese Imperial Household Law bans any girl from becoming emperor. The law says: "The Imperial throne of Japan shall be succeeded to by male descendants in the male line of Imperi Ancestors." Since there are no male grandchildren Emperor Akihito, the law should be changed to all the baby girl to inherit the throne and carry on Imperial family line. A female Japanese emperor also be a fantastic symbol of modern times and t equality of men and women.

If the law is not changed, the Imperial dynasty could come to an end after 2,661 uninte years. But it's important for this family dynas

Fact #1:
Here's why.

keep going. It's the longest recorded dynasty in the world, and it's a key element of Japanese culture. The emperor is the respected symbol of Japan, representing the goodwill of the people and the country's fascinating ancient culture. Meeting with delegations from other countries and participating in festivals and celebrations, the emperor links past centuries with the present for the people of Japan. This continuous history is a source of pride to many Japanese people.

The person who becomes emperor should also be the people's favorite. In a recent poll, approximately 86% of Japanese polled supported the idea of having a female emperor. The Japanese people already admire Aiko's parents and grandparents and are confident that they will raise her to be an admirable ruler.

Fact #2:
More proof!

Finally, Japan is very capable of blending old traditions with modern ideas. Japan has shown that it's open to the idea that women should have the same opportunities as men by appointing a Minister of Gender Equality. Japan also had eight female emperors in its distant past, and many other countries, such as Britain, Denmark, and the Netherlands, have had successful female leaders.

Fact #3:
Convinced yet?

Cultural traditions are significant and valuable to the Japanese, but this is the modern world, a time for women to be recognized as equal to men. By allowing the baby girl to inherit the throne, Japan will be honoring past traditions and embracing modern ideas. A female emperor would be a bright symbol for all to see.

Here's a recap
to end on a
strong note.

Paper Trail

Don't try to write an entire research paper in one day. Divide up the work and tackle one part at a time. Here are some steps to help you get organized.

1 Get a great idea.

Pick a topic that you can care about. Your enthusiasm will show—and your paper won't be such a chore to write!

2. Get the scoop.

Collect all the info you can find. Mine the library, the Internet, a local science center or museum. Dig deeper into your topic by asking questions, then search out the answers. Use index cards to keep track of what you know. Hint: Write one important idea or concept on each card. Be sure to write your source on every card.

3.

Organize what you want to say.

Shuffle your note cards and decide how to present the information. Then make an outline by listing the info in the order in which you want to write about it.

Q. How will you present your info? Pick one:

a. Chronologically:
Put information in the order in which it happens.

b. Order of Importance:
Rank the information and put the most important fact either first or last.

c. Cause & Effect:
Describe a problem, explain what causes it and what results from it, and offer solutions.

d. Compare & Contrast:
Write about how two subjects or ideas are alike or different.

4.

Make a mess!

Now you're ready to write the first draft. Use your note cards or outline as a guide. Don't worry about spelling or grammar or neatness.
Hint: Skip every other line or use double-spacing so you'll be able to write in changes easily.

5.

Make it better!

Put on your editor's cap and read your first draft out loud. Decide what should stay in the paper and what should go. Mark places where you think the writing could be stronger. Make notes in the margins. Go back for more info if necessary. See the writer's checklist on the next page for other important questions to ask yourself.

Grade Yourself

Time to edit your paper! Read it back to yourself a couple of times with these questions in mind.

REPORT CARD

✓	
	Did I follow the teacher's directions for the assignment?
	Did I use the same verb tense all the way through?
	Do I have an interesting hook—a good way to catch the reader's attention?
	Did I use strong nouns and verbs, and give details that stick?
	Did I slip into passive voice? (If so, change it to active.)

Passive	Active
The marigolds were planted by Lucy.	Lucy planted the marigolds.
The stage makeup was applied by Lon.	Lon applied the stage makeup.
Music was written by Mozart.	Mozart wrote music.

	Did I spell and punctuate correctly?
	Do my subjects and verbs agree?
	Do my pronouns refer back to the correct nouns?
	Do all my paragraphs support the big idea, or premise? (Make sure that you stick to the subject at hand. Delete extra sentences that repeat info or don't support your main idea.)
	Did I use a variety of long and short sentences to keep things interesting?
	Did I use the same word too many times? Look in a synonym finder for replacements.
	Do I transition, or move smoothly, from one paragraph to the next?
	Did I put quotation marks around direct quotes and note my sources? Books, encyclopedias, Web sites, and other sources of info are copyrighted. That means someone else owns the words. You can use them but only if you put them in quotation marks and note where you got them from. Better yet, you could try to put the info into your own words.
	Does my conclusion pack some punch and summarize what I've talked about?

comments

If you're working on a computer, print out your paper before editing. It's easier to catch errors on a hard copy than on the screen. And don't rely on spellcheck and grammar-check programs to find all your mistakes. Use your own eyes, ears, and head!

Mark It Up

Use proofreading symbols to mark changes on your paper.

- (tr) transpose, or switch the order of the words or letters
- ⁋ start a new paragraph
- (ital) italicize
- (cap) make uppercase
- (lc) make lowercase
- (ins) insert a word or punctuation mark
- ℰ delete and close up
- ⊙ insert period
- (stet) stet, or let original text stand
  (aka, "I changed my mind" or "Oops! It was right to begin with")

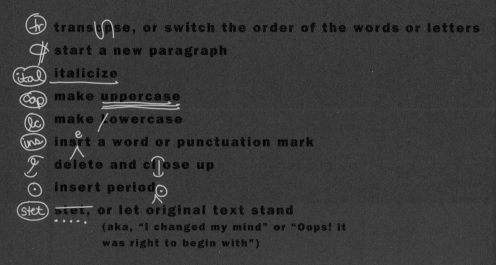

Marigolds

(tr) My project science is on whether marigold flowers growed best in soil, sand, or clay. my hypothesis is that the marigold plant thrives best in soil. I think this hypotheses is true be cause soil is what you usually use to grow flowers and plants, and if watered and weeded regularly, plants and flowers grow really well good in soil.

Oops!

We forgot to proofread this page before we sent the book to press!
See if you can catch all of our mistakes.

Flamenco Dancing

The origin of the word *flamenco* is uncler. Some people say it had came from the gypsy word fleming, which meaned "outsider." Since the gypsys were shunned always everywhere they went, it is to believe that they named their dance after themselves—outsiders. no one really knows. It turned out that the gypsies settled in southern france because they were runned out of many other countries. The dance itself has many influences, such as arabian asian, african, and middle-Eastern. The elements of the dance all come together as Flamenco when the gypsies began using Spanish movements such as foot stomping and other technicks.

How many errors did you catch?
Compare your test against this one to see if you have an eagle eye!

Flamenco Dancing

The origin of the word *flamenco* is unclear.

Some people say it had came from the gypsy word

(ital) fleming, which meaned "outsider." Since the gyp-

sys were shunned always everywhere they went, it

is to believe that they named their dance after

themselves—outsiders. no one really knows. It

turned out that the gypsies settled in southern

france because they were runned out of many other

countries. The dance itself has many influences,

such as arabian asian, african, and middle-

Eastern. The elements of the dance all come

together as Flamenco when the gypsies began

using Spanish movements such as foot stomping and

other technicks.

If you caught . . .

15 or more mistakes
You've got an eagle eye! Keep up the good work.

8–14 mistakes
You're on your way to making a better grade! Brush up on your grammar and spelling with the Get-it-Right guide.

7 or fewer mistakes
Need to know what to look out for? Visit the Get-it-Right guide on the following pages for common mistakes, punctuation rules, and more.

Get-It-Right Guide

Stamp out mistakes! Keep this quick-reference grammar and spelling guide at your side when proofreading papers.

Trusty Transitions

Need to get from one paragraph to the next smoothly? Try these:

To show time: About, after, at, meanwhile, next week, as soon as, when, immediately	**To compare two things:** in the same way, similarly, likewise, like	**To show location:** above, across, among, around, behind, below, by, inside, throughout	**To contrast things:** but, on the other hand, however, although, otherwise
To conclude or summarize: in short, to sum it up, as a result	**To add information:** again, also, for example, for instance	**To make more clear:** in other words	**To emphasize a point:** again, to repeat, for this reason

Overused Words

boring • dumb • fun • great • interesting • stuff • things

Pick your brain—or browse the thesaurus—for replacement words that are more specific or unique.

Get-It-Right Guide

Tricky Irregular Verbs
Watch out for verbs that change spelling for different tenses.

Present	Past	Past Participle
		(have, has, & had + verb)
am	was, were	been
arise	arose	arisen
begin	began	begun
bring	brought	brought
catch	caught	caught
choose	chose	chosen
come	came	come
do	did	done
draw	drew	drawn
drink	drank	drunk
eat	ate	eaten
fall	fell	fallen
find	found	found
fly	flew	flown
forgive	forgave	forgiven
freeze	froze	frozen
give	gave	given
go	went	gone
grow	grew	grown
have	had	had
hide	hid	hidden, hid
know	knew	known
lay (object)	laid	laid
lie (person)	lay	lain
lie (fib)	lied	lied
ride	rode	ridden
ring	rang	rung
see	saw	seen
shrink	shrank	shrunk
sink	sank	sunk
sleep	slept	slept
slink	slunk	slunk
speak	spoke	spoken
spring	sprang	sprung
swim	swam	swum
sting	stung	stung
strike	struck	struck
swell	swelled	swollen
take	took	taken
teach	taught	taught
tear	tore	torn
think	thought	thought
throw	threw	thrown
wear	wore	worn
write	wrote	written

Commonly Misspelled Words
Don't get stung by the spelling bee!

absence	occurred
academic	original
accomplish	outrageous
arctic	parallel
basically	perform
believe	permission
brilliant	prejudice
cemetery	quiet
chosen	quite
column	quizzes
conqueror	receive
definitely	recognize
describe	recommend
despair	sandwich
disagree	schedule
dissatisfied	secretary
embarrass	separate
eligible	several
entrance	temperature
environment	tragedy
February	tries
foreign	truly
friend	unanimous
grammar	unnecessarily
guard	usually
guidance	villain
height	weird
humorous	
illiterate	
imaginary	
incredible	
infinite	
laboratory	
lightning	
loneliness	
literature	
maneuver	
marriage	
mathematics	
mischievous	
occur	

Homonyms & Other Commonly Confused Words
Use these sentences to help you choose the right word.

accept, except	I **accept** your excuse, **except** for the part about the dog eating it.
advise, advice	I **advise** you to use Daddy's **advice** when cooking new recipes.
allowed, aloud	She finally **allowed** me to read her poem **aloud.**
all ready, already	I'm **all ready** to go **already.**
ate, eight	Billy **ate eight** ice cream cones for breakfast.
bored, board	I was **bored** so I volunteered to write on the **board.**
brake, break	Make sure the **brake** on your scooter doesn't **break.**
bye, buy, by	I said **bye** to my mom so I could **buy** her roses **by** the roadside.
chose, choose	I **chose** the purple platforms. Which shoes will you **choose?**
course, coarse	Of **course,** sandpaper is **coarse!**
cot, caught	The **cot** got **caught** between the door and the wall.
dessert, desert	My **dessert** tasted like the **desert**—dry and gritty.
die, dye	You won't **die** if you wear a tie-**dye** shirt just once!
flour, flower	You don't need **flour** to grow a **flower.**
gait, gate	The horse trotted at a fast **gait** toward the **gate.**
heel, heal	I can't wait until the blisters on my **heel heal.**
hey, hay	**Hey,** Harry, did you bring the **hay** for the hayride?
it's, its	**It's** not unusual for a bus to take **its** time.
led, lead	My teacher **led** me to where the pencil **lead** was broken on the floor.
loose, lose	If the lizard gets **loose,** you may **lose** him.
made, maid	Is your bed **made,** or do I have to be your **maid?**
medal, metal	The winner will receive a **medal** made out of **metal.**
miner, minor	The **miner** found a **minor** piece of gold.
past, passed	In the **past,** Margaret always **passed** her spelling tests.
piece, peace	Cut a **piece** of pie and declare **peace.**
plain, plane	As I stood on the **plain,** a **plane** flew overhead.
principal, principle	The **principal** stuck to his **principles.**
read, red	Have you **read** the words written in **red?**
seen, scene	The movie star insists on being **seen** in each **scene.**
stationary, stationery	"Remain **stationary,**" I wrote on my new **stationery.**
than, then	I'd rather bike **than** walk, because **then** we'll have time to swim.
their, there, they're	**Their** coats used to be over **there,** but now **they're** over here!
threw, through	Who **threw** my shoe **through** the window?
two, to, too	The **two** of you need **to** go home, **too!**
weigh, way	Now Billy is going to **weigh way** too much!
wait, weight	Please **wait** until the **weight** of the package is determined.
where, wear	**Where** should I **wear** my new sweater?
whether, weather	I don't know **whether** or not bad **weather** is coming.
whose, who's	**Whose** present is on the table, and **who's** going to open it?
you're, your	**You're** not going to **your** recital unless you practice.

Get-It-Right Guide

Period

To complete a statement or thought:
I wish I could fly to the moon.

For initials or abbreviations:
C.J. has an appointment with Dr. Walker.

As decimal points:
The earthquake registered a 2.3 on the Richter scale.

Comma

To keep a series of two or more words from crashing into each other:
I love cherries, peaches, and plums!

Between two clauses or to indicate a pause:
If you go swimming, Mom will pick you up.

Before or after quotation marks:
She smiled and said, "Thanks!"
"No problem," I replied.

Between dates and in large numbers:
July 8, 2003
28,000

Italics

Book titles:
Have you read *The Hobbit*?

Magazine or newspaper names:
The new issue of *National Geographic* came today.

Movie or TV show titles:
We watched *Willy Wonka and the Chocolate Factory* last night.
If your're writing by hand, underline the words you would italicize.

Capitalization

First word in a sentence:
Let's go!

Names of people, cities, and states:
Can Jessie go to Chicago with Mom and me?

Days, months, and holidays:
I think Christmas falls on a Saturday this year.

Important words in a title:
Let's call this story "French Fries and Friends," not "Dinner with a Clown."

Apostrophe

To show ownership:
Kari's shoes needed polishing.
The children's bikes are muddy.

In contractions to show where letters are left out:
It's time to go or we'll miss the plane.

Exclamation Point

To express feeling or show emphasis:
You promised!
Hurry up!
Yowza!
(Don't use too many in a row, or they won't pack as much punch.)

Quotation Marks

To show dialogue, or words that are spoken:
"Can you come over for dinner?" Sissy asked.
"Chelsea," said her mother, "your pancakes are ready."
Commas, question marks, and exclamation points go inside the quotation marks.
For titles of songs, poems, or chapters in a book:
I recited "The Village Blacksmith" in class today.
We sang "YMCA" at the ballgame.

Question Mark

To beg an answer:
Are you happy today?

To show doubt:
You don't really want to eat that last piece of cake, do you?

Sample Bibliography

Follow these examples to let your teacher know where you got all that great info for your paper!

Format tips:
- List sources in alphabetical order.
- Begin the first line of each entry at the left margin, then indent any extra lines.

Book with One Author
DiCamillo, Kate. *Because of Winn-Dixie.* Cambridge MA: Candlewick Press, 2000.
Creech, Sharon. *Heartbeat.* New York: Harper Collins, 2004.
Blume, Judy. *Double Fudge.* New York: Dutton Children's Books, 2002.

Book with More than One Author
Rhatigan, Joe, and Newcomb, Rain. *Prize-Winning Science Fair Projects for Curious Kids.* New York: Lark Books, 2004

Magazine Article
Turner, Pamela S. "California, Here We Come." *Cobblestone* (May 2005): 8–11.

Encyclopedia Article: Print and CD-ROM
"Human Spaceflight." *Compton's Encyclopedia.* 2004 edition.

Films & Videos
New York: Sunshine and Shadow, Episode Three: 1865–1898. PBS Home Video, Burbank, CA, 1999.

Interview
Rowling, J.K. Telephone interview. London, England, April 22, 2005.

Web Site
"Clues from the Past: Trapped in Amber." Online. May 31, 2005 National Geographic Kids [http://www.nationalgeographic.com/ngkids/9609/amber/index.html].

Great Presentations

Neatness Counts!

When revisions are done, type or write the final draft of your paper with all the new changes added.

Cover Page

Put your name, the date, and the name of the class on the cover.

Use a bigger type size for the title, and center it in the middle of the page.

A spot of art makes your paper more inviting!

Lucy Madden-Lunsford
November 13, 2001
Social Studies

Flamenco Dancing

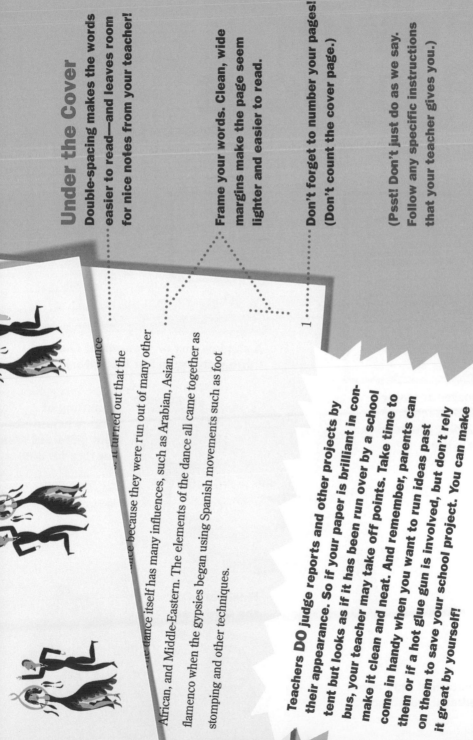

Under the Cover

Double-spacing makes the words easier to read—and leaves room for nice notes from your teacher!

Frame your words. Clean, wide margins make the page seem lighter and easier to read.

Don't forget to number your pages! (Don't count the cover page.)

(Psst! Don't just do as we say. Follow any specific instructions that your teacher gives you.)

1

...dance

...t turned out that the

...ce because they were run out of many other

...e dance itself has many influences, such as Arabian, Asian, African, and Middle-Eastern. The elements of the dance all came together as flamenco when the gypsies began using Spanish movements such as foot stomping and other techniques.

Teachers **DO** judge reports and other projects by their appearance. So if your paper is brilliant in content but looks as if it has been run over by a school bus, your teacher may take off points. Take time to make it clean and neat. And remember, parents can come in handy when you want to run ideas past them or if a hot glue gun is involved, but don't rely on them to save your school project. You can make it great by yourself!

Power Projects

to run by your teacher first!

Bring your paper to life by presenting the info in fun, creative ways.

A shadow box or diorama of Marie Curie working in her laboratory

A poster of major snake species, including anacondas and rattlers

A painting of famous scientists from different eras meeting for dinner

Flashcards of the Civil War

A historical play about medieval weddings

Idea Deck

Can't think of anything to write? Not an idea in sight? Punch out these cards, shuffle them well, and pick one to get a creative spark. Keep the deck by your side so that you can deal yourself an idea whenever writer's block strikes.

Every Picture Tells a Story

Woof!

Make a Prediction

Think
It's O.K. if you just sit and **do nothing** but think for a while. Eventually nothing will lead to something!

How Bad Can It Be?
Write the **worst story ever written.** It can have flying pigs that sing or skinny truck drivers who make you eat onion casseroles. The only rule is that it has to be terrible! You'll have so much fun letting go and writing a truly terrible story that some really creative ideas are bound to show up.

ASTROLOGY
Forecast for Tuesday

...rthday! In the next year... This year is about step-...boundaries. You're being ...y new things because ...n your old routine. Trust ...ritical woman who loves ...netimes-strict man who ...n soar.
...vantage, check the day's ...e easiest day, the most
...21-...9, Today ...s like everybody wants ...really
...expect mo...th you can give ...you holding back?

Strike a Poem
Grab the newspaper and find an article. Read it and **circle words** that strike your fancy. Copy them onto a piece of paper. You just might have a poem.

Get the Scoop!

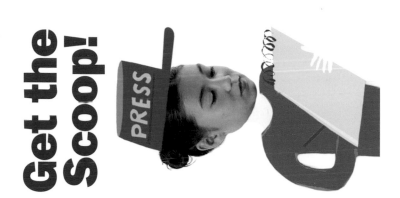

Pretend you're a reporter covering the family beat and you need to write a story by 5 P.M. Find someone to interview. Ask your brother why he came home grumpy. Discover what Mom's making for dinner. Quiz the dog on why he always knocks over his water bowl. Write down what family members have to say, then go **file a report.**

How Bad Can It Be?

Write the **worst story ever written.** It can have flying pigs that sing or skinny truck drivers who make you eat onion casseroles. The only rule is that it has to be terrible! You'll have so much fun letting go and writing a truly terrible story that some really creative ideas are bound to show up.

Every Picture Tells a Story

Cut out two pictures from a magazine or find two postcards. Place them beside each other on your desk. The first picture is the beginning of your story. The second picture is the end of your story. **Write what happens** in the middle.

Take a Walk!

Grab your idea notebook and take a walk. Pay attention to what you **see**, **smell**, and **hear:** Raindrops and wet leaves. Squeaky shoes. The mail carrier whistling while she works. A cacophony of cawing crows. Jot down random thoughts and let them swim around your brain until an idea takes hold.

Be a Critic

Did you just get a new CD or see a new movie? **Write a review.** What did you love about it? What did you hate about it? Is it the best ever or the worst yet? Explain why. Dream up a rating system—stars, bananas, thumbs, whatever—to rank where it falls on your fave-o-meter.

Strike a Poem

Grab the newspaper and find an article. Read it and **circle words** that strike your fancy. Copy them onto a piece of paper. You just might have a poem!

ASTROLOGY

Forecast for Tuesday

Happy Birthday! In the next year of your life: This year is about stepping past old boundaries. You're being pushed to try new things, because you've outgrown your old routine. Trust a sometimes-critical woman who loves you, and a sometimes-strict man who believes you can soar.

To get the advantage, check the day's rating: 10 is the easiest day, 0 the most challenging.

Aries (March 21–) Today is a 6... See... like everybody wants your time and att... expect mo... really ...p... you holding back? Tau... can give, or ...

Listen In

Go to a public place—park, store, restaurant—and listen in on other people's conversations (just don't be obvious or rude about it!). Take notes about what's being said. Pay attention to unusual accents, slang, and the tone of the voices. How many times do the people say "cool"? Are they excited or bored? Then pretend you're in a play, add your own dialogue, and create an ending.

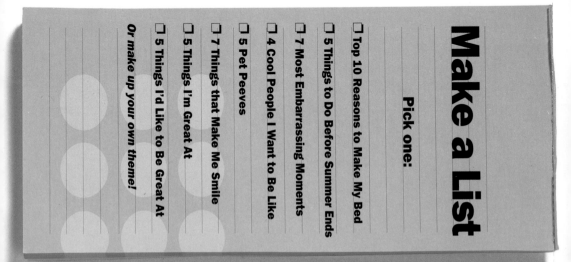

Make a List

Pick one:

☐ Top 10 Reasons to Make My Bed

☐ 5 Things to Do Before Summer Ends

☐ 7 Most Embarrassing Moments

☐ 4 Cool People I Want to Be Like

☐ 5 Pet Peeves

☐ 7 Things that Make Me Smile

☐ 5 Things I'm Great At

☐ 5 Things I'd Like to Be Great At

Or make up your own theme!

Dance!

Get into character by playing your leading gal's favorite music. Does she like disco? Or boy bands? Turn up the volume and **twirl** around the room as she might do. Get funky or do the chicken dance! Then write about how your character feels jamming to her favorite music.

"I'd Like to Thank . . ."

Congratulations!

You've just won the **Golden Pencil Award.** Write your acceptance speech.

Here's How

Pick something you're really good at, like popping popcorn or scoring that coveted backseat on the bus. Write down how you do it **step-by-step**.

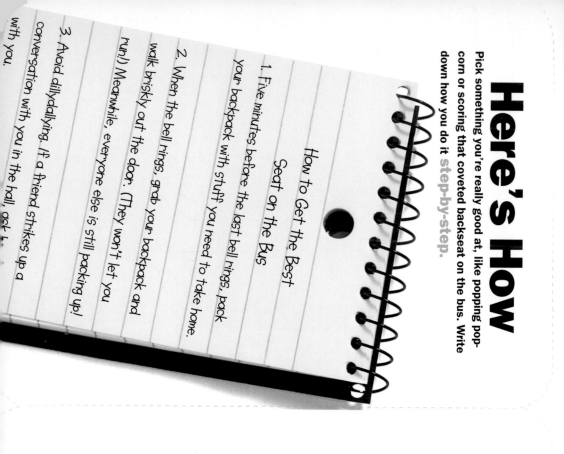

How to Get the Best
Seat on the Bus

1. Five minutes before the last bell rings, pack your backpack with stuff you need to take home.

2. When the bell rings, grab your backpack and walk briskly out the door. (They won't let you run!) Meanwhile, everyone else is still packing up!

3. Avoid dillydallying. If a friend strikes up a conversation with you in the hall, ask h...
with you.

Woof!

Imagine you are your dog—or your cat, or your baby sister—and write down what she must be thinking right now. How would she see the world? Work it into a story.

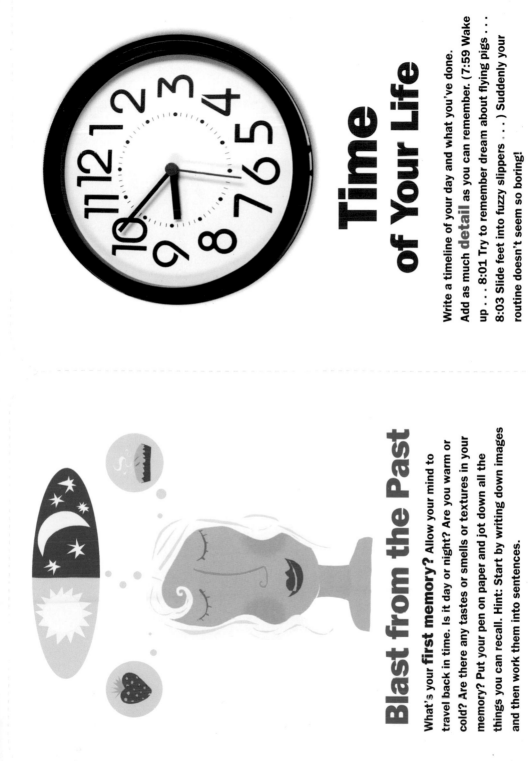

Time of Your Life

Write a timeline of your day and what you've done. Add as much **detail** as you can remember. (7:59 Wake up . . . 8:01 Try to remember dream about flying pigs . . . 8:03 Slide feet into fuzzy slippers . . .) Suddenly your routine doesn't seem so boring!

Blast from the Past

What's your **first memory?** Allow your mind to travel back in time. Is it day or night? Are you warm or cold? Are there any tastes or smells or textures in your memory? Put your pen on paper and jot down all the things you can recall. Hint: Start by writing down images and then work them into sentences.

Think

It's O.K. if you just sit
and **do nothing**
but think for a while.
Eventually nothing
will lead to something!

Make a prediction

What will you be when you grow up? What kind of car will
you drive on your 16th birthday? What will your mom do
when she finds out about that stain on the carpet? Who
will your brother pick on next? Look into your crystal ball
and **predict** what will happen in the future—near or far!